King Alfred's
Winchester

Martial Rose Library
Tel: 01962 827306

KT-147-643

2 5 APR 2005

- 4 NOV 2003

2 4 MAY 2005

1 8 DEC 2003

1 7 JUN 2005
- 7 NOV 2009

1 7 JUN 2011

2 6 JAN 2004

2 5 OCT 2004

WITHDRAWN FROM
THE LIBRARY
UNIVERSITY OF
WINCHESTER

To be returned on or before the day marked above, subject to recall.

KA 0272733 1

PUBLISHED BY THE PRESS SYNDICATE OF THE UNIVERSITY OF CAMBRIDGE
The Pitt Building, Trumpington Street, Cambridge, United Kingdom

CAMBRIDGE UNIVERSITY PRESS
The Edinburgh Building, Cambridge CB2 2RU, UK
40 West 20th Street, New York, NY 10011-4211, USA
477 Williamstown Road, Port Melbourne, VIC 3207, Australia
Ruiz de Alarcón 13, 28014 Madrid, Spain
Dock House, The Waterfront, Cape Town 8001, South Africa

http://www.cambridge.org

© Cambridge University Press 1999

First published 1999
Eighth Printing 2003

This book is in copyright. Subject to statutory exception and
to the provisions of relevant collective licensing agreements,
no reproduction of any part may take place without
the written permission of Cambridge University Press.

Printed in Italy by Legoprint S.p.A

Typeset in 12/15 Adobe Garamond [CE]
Illustrations by Gary Taylor

ISBN 0 521 65615 X

KING ALFRED'S COLLEGE
WINCHESTER

02727331 | 428.6 CAM.

Contents

3

KING ALFRED'S COLLEGE
LIBRARY

People in the story

Frank Wormold: a writer.

Teresa Wormold: a lawyer and Frank's wife.

Mel Parks: a Hollywood producer.

Chip: a computer.

A postman.

Chapter 1 *"Every Morning"*

'I'm leaving now,' Teresa said.

I looked up from the newspaper. I was in the kitchen, at the table.

'I'm leaving,' Teresa, my wife, said again. She stood at the kitchen table and looked down at me. I looked at my watch. It was eight o'clock in the morning. Time for Teresa, my wife, to go to work. She was a lawyer, a very good lawyer. And she was beautiful.

'What are you going to do today?' Teresa asked. 'Don't go back to bed! Why don't you go out and look for a job?'

'Oh no,' I thought. 'Eight o'clock in the morning, and she's telling me to get a job.'

'But I've got a job,' I said, for about the thousandth time. 'I'm a writer.'

'But you never finish your books! You begin lots of books, but you never finish them.'

She was right. I write by hand in small notebooks – I've got lots of notebooks under the bed – but I don't finish the books.

And sometimes I don't work. Sometimes I sit all day with a white piece of paper and a pen and write nothing. Sometimes I sleep all morning and then I get up and watch television all afternoon.

'You need a real job,' Teresa said. 'We must have more money!'

'Why?' I asked. 'Why must we have more money?'

'We need money to buy things,' she said. 'You need new clothes. Look at your old clothes!' I had an old pullover and jeans on. She had expensive black clothes on.

'There's nothing wrong with my clothes,' I answered. 'My jeans are a little dirty, but I can wash them.'

'You do need new clothes!' Teresa said. 'And I want a nice car. And we need a new television!'

I closed my eyes. Why was Teresa like this in the mornings?

'Open your eyes! Don't go to sleep,' Teresa said. 'I'm talking to you.'

'Look,' I answered. 'I'm not sleeping. I'm thinking. Anyway, you don't read my books,' I said.

'I read the first half of "Every Morning",' Teresa said. 'I liked it.'

Oh, yes, I thought. That was two years ago. Teresa read the first half of one of my books called "Every Morning".

It was about a young man in London. She sent the book to all the big London and Hollywood film makers. The film makers didn't answer. And I didn't finish the book.

'Good,' I answered.

'I think I'm going to be home late this evening,' she said. 'There's a lot to do at work.'

'Goodbye,' I answered. 'Have a nice day.'

Teresa closed the door. She didn't say goodbye.

I stood up. Then I saw something black on the floor. It was Teresa's laptop computer. I opened the door but

Teresa wasn't there. I went and sat in a chair in front of the television. I thought about Teresa. She was thirty years old. I was thirty years old. She had dark hair and eyes. I had dark hair and eyes. She was one metre eighty. I was one metre eighty. But Teresa liked to work with computers and I didn't like computers. I liked to write with an old pen. She made a lot of money in her job and I made nothing. And now she was angry with me – again.

I closed my eyes and went to sleep.

Chapter 2 *The letter*

I heard a noise. What was it? I opened my eyes and looked at my watch. It was nine o'clock. There was someone at the front door. I got up slowly and went to the door.

It was the postman. He had some letters in his hand. He looked at my hair.

'Just got up, Mr Wormold?' the postman said. 'I got up six hours ago.'

I didn't answer. I was half-asleep.

'There's a letter for you,' the postman said. 'It's from the USA. Write your name here, please.'

I wrote my name on the postman's paper and took the letter.

'Thank you,' I said and closed the door. I went into the kitchen and looked at the letter. It was big and blue. At the top it said: 'Rogers, Tannenbaum and Schutz, Attorneys, Hollywood, California, USA.'

'American lawyers!' I thought. Was the letter for Teresa and not for me? But my name was on the front.

Then I opened the letter and read it.

Rogers, Tannenbaum and Schutz Attorneys

Hollywood, California U.S.A.

Dear Mr Wormold,

We work for Mel Parks of the MegaMonster Movie Corporation.

Mr Parks read the first half of your book "Every Morning". He likes it very much and wants to read the second half of the story. He also wants to meet you and talk about making a movie of the book.

Mr Parks is in London on March 29th and 30th. He is staying at the Waldorf Hotel. Please telephone him there.

Please do not talk to anyone else about making a movie of "Every Morning".

Yours truly,

R. Steinback

I put the letter on the table and smiled to myself. An answer at last, two years after Teresa sent the first half of my book "Every Morning" to all the Hollywood film makers. The American word 'movie' was much nicer than the British word 'film'. And today was March 29th!

I found the phone number of the Waldorf Hotel in the telephone book. Then I telephoned Mel Parks.

'Hi, Mel Parks here.'

'Erm. Mr Parks. You don't know me,' I said slowly. 'My name's Wormold, Frank Wormold.'

'Mr Wormold!' Mel Parks answered in a loud voice. 'Or can I call you Frank? It's very good to talk to you! How are you?'

'Fine, thank you,' I said.

'Say, Frank,' Mel Parks said. 'Why don't we have lunch today?'

'Yes,' I said. 'How nice.'

'OK,' Mel Parks said. 'See you here at the Waldorf at twelve thirty.'

'Right,' I said.

'And bring the second half of your story "Every Morning" with you,' Mel Parks said.

I put the telephone down. There was no second half of "Every Morning". I looked at my watch. It was half past nine. I got a notebook and my old pen and started writing.

When I looked at my watch again it was eleven o'clock. The second half of "Every Morning" was not finished, but it was time to change my clothes. I wanted to look good because the Waldorf was a very famous hotel.

I put on my best clothes. A new brown shirt and dark brown trousers and a jacket. Then I left the flat and got into the lift.

'Sixth floor. Going down,' the lift said. It was a talking lift.

'Yes, I know,' I replied.

When I got out of the lift I took a bus to Piccadilly Circus and walked to the Waldorf Hotel.

Chapter 3 *Mel Parks*

Lots of rich people come to the Waldorf Hotel. I looked at myself in a shop window. I didn't look rich.

Mel Parks was by the front door of the hotel. He did look rich. He was short and fat. He had a green suit and a big red tie.

'Well, Frank,' Mel Parks said in his loud voice. 'Good to see you!'

'Hello, Mr Parks,' I said with a small smile.

'Don't call me "Mr Parks",' he answered. 'Call me Mel!'

'Hello, Mel,' I said.

'Let's get some lunch,' Mel said.

The Waldorf Hotel restaurant was very good. Lots of rich, beautiful people and lots of rich, beautiful food. Mel and I had caviar, and lobster and champagne. Lots of champagne. I was very happy. Mel liked me and Mel liked my story.

Then Mel said: 'Hey, Frank. I loved the first half of your book. Did you bring the second half of the book with you?'

'Er, no,' I said. 'I'm writing it again. I want to make it better.' I didn't want to tell Mel the book wasn't finished.

Mel looked at me. He looked unhappy.

'Oh no,' he said. 'I wanted to take it to California with me.'

KING ALFRED'S COLLEGE LIBRARY

12

'I'm sorry,' I answered. 'You see I write very slowly. I write by hand.'

'Don't tell me!' Mel said. 'I know. Your writing isn't easy to read. Why don't you use a computer?'

'I ... I ...' I started to answer. I didn't want to tell Mel I didn't like computers.

'Hey, Frank,' Mel said. 'Is it money? That's easy. MegaMonster wants your book. You're going to be a rich man. You're going to be famous. Let's say we give you $100,000 now.'

I looked at Mel. My mouth opened. I couldn't speak.

'Oh,' Mel said quickly. '$100,000 is too little, is it? Let's say $200,000, then.'

I looked at Mel again. My mouth was still open. I still couldn't speak. $200,000 was so much money.

'OK,' Mel said quickly again. 'And a computer. You need a computer. You're going to have the best computer in London. OK?'

'Oh,' I said slowly.

Mel took my hand. 'Good. Let's get the computer today. And you're going to finish the book and give it to me this week. All right?' He smiled.

'Yes,' I said. I didn't know what to do or think. $200,000! I was rich!

We had some more champagne. Mel talked and talked. I didn't listen much. I thought about $200,000.

After lunch Mel and I took a taxi to a big computer shop. Mel went into the shop first and Mel did all the talking. 'Right,' Mel said. 'I want the biggest and the best PC you have. I want lots of RAM, I want a colour printer and I want a fast modem.'

'Mel,' I said slowly. 'I don't think I need a colour printer. I write books.'

Mel looked at me. 'Yes, you do,' he said in a loud voice.

'OK. And what's RAM?' I asked in a quiet voice. 'Why do I need lots of it?'

'Memory,' Mel said. 'RAM is the memory in a computer.'

'And a modem?' I asked. 'What's a modem?'

'With a modem your computer can talk to the telephone,' Mel said. 'You write your book on the computer. Then you send it to me by e-mail.'

'What's e-mail?' I asked.

'The Internet,' Mel said. 'You can send letters by computer all over the world quickly.'

I didn't ask any more questions. Mel bought lots of things for the computer.

Then we got into a taxi with the computer things.

I sat in the taxi and thought about the morning. 'We're going to be rich,' I said to myself. 'Teresa and I are going to be rich. We're going to have lots of money. Teresa's going to be happy. And I'm going to be happy. Teresa's not going to be angry with me now!'

Chapter 4 *Chip*

Mel put the computer on a table in the living room. He put it by the telephone. Then he did something to the computer and a face came on the screen.

It was a woman's face. 'Hi!' the woman said. 'I'm Chip, talking to you from MegaMonster Movies in California. I'm going to help you with your computer. Type "Help!" on the keyboard and wait.'

'You're OK now,' said Mel. 'I'm going back to the Waldorf. I'll ring you tomorrow to see how things are going.' Then he left.

I typed 'Help!' and waited. Chip's face went away. The computer made a noise. It was like 'Ping!' Then Chip's face came back.

Hi! I'm Chip.

'Hi!' Chip said with a big smile. 'I'm now inside your computer. When you need help type "Help!" I can help you use the computer, and help with your spelling and grammar. And lots more things.'

'What things?' I typed.

'Wait and see,' Chip said.

Chip was a very good teacher. With Chip's help I learned to use the computer. It was easy and it was fun! I worked all afternoon and into the evening. And I was happy to work with the computer.

'Why didn't I do this before?' I asked myself. 'Why did I write with a pen? Why was I afraid of computers? Writing like this is quick and easy.'

Then I heard the telephone. It was Teresa.

'I'm sorry, Frank,' Teresa said. 'I'm still at work. I'm not coming home tonight. I'm going to stay in a hotel.'

'Teresa,' I said. 'Listen, I want to tell you something. We're going to be . . .'

'I'm sorry, Frank,' Teresa said. 'I can't talk now. Tell me tomorrow. Goodbye.'

Teresa didn't want to talk. She was still angry with me. So I didn't tell her about MegaMonster Movies, the computer and Chip. I worked on the computer until midnight. I didn't have anything to eat or drink.

The next day Mel Parks telephoned.

'How are you, Frank?' he said. 'Everything OK?'

'Fine, thank you, Mel,' I answered. 'It's a very good computer. I'm learning to use it.'

'Great,' Mel said. 'I'm leaving for California now. Send me the book by e-mail this week.'

I put down the telephone and started work. "Every Morning" was a story about Joe, a young newspaper man in London and the people he knew.

First I typed in the first half of the story from my notebook. I worked and worked. I didn't think about Chip. Then the computer went 'Ping!' and there was Chip on the screen.

'Well, Frank,' Chip said. She didn't smile. 'Don't you want me to help? You're not asking for help.'

I wanted to be nice to Chip. So I typed, 'Sorry, Chip. Please help with spelling.'

The computer made a noise. Then Chip came back. 'Color not colour,' it said on the screen.

'No, Chip,' I typed. 'Colour is British English. Color is American.'

'I know what is right,' Chip replied. 'The spelling is color.'

'OK,' I typed. Chip went away. I wasn't happy with the spelling. 'But the movie is American,' I thought, 'so it was OK to have American spelling.'

An hour later there was a 'Ping!' and Chip came back.

'Frank,' she said. 'Let me help you. Let me help with your story.'

'How can you help?' I asked.

'Well,' Chip replied. 'I don't like Joe's name. Let's call him Red.'

'But red's a colour,' I typed.

'Color,' replied Chip. 'Red's a good name.'

'I don't think so,' I typed. 'And it's my book.'

'I know best,' Chip answered.

I tried to change Chip's changes, but I couldn't do anything. So I started work again. I worked all morning. I didn't have any breakfast. I wrote and wrote. Sometimes Chip came on the screen with more 'help'.

I was very thirsty. Then I heard something in the kitchen. It was a loud noise. There was someone in the kitchen! I got up and walked slowly to the kitchen door. I opened the door quickly. There was no-one there. But in the microwave there was a cup of hot coffee. Wow! I wanted a cup of coffee, but I was afraid. Was there someone else in the flat? I looked in all the rooms. I was the only person there. I took the coffee and went back to the

computer. I typed 'Help!' There was a 'Ping!' and Chip came on the screen.

'Can I help?' she asked.

'This cup of coffee,' I typed. 'Where did it come from?'

Chip said nothing.

'Come on,' I typed. 'Tell me.'

'Drink the coffee, and start working again,' Chip said.

I wanted to finish the story so I did what Chip said. At two in the afternoon I heard another noise in the kitchen. I got up and ran into the kitchen. There was no-one there. I slowly opened the microwave door. In the microwave there was a hot meal – spaghetti. I love spaghetti. I sat down at the table and ate it. This time I didn't look in all the rooms.

I went back to the computer and typed 'Help!' When Chip came on the screen I typed 'Thank you'. She said 'I hope it was a nice lunch.'

'It was great,' I said with a smile.

I worked all afternoon. Then Chip came on the screen.

'Let's have the book in New York,' she said. 'Red now lives in New York, not London. New York's much better than London.'

'No,' I typed. But when I looked at the screen I saw the book was now in New York.

I wasn't happy but I needed to finish the story. I wrote and wrote. Then I heard a noise. There was someone at the door. I opened the door. There were two men in white coats with a big television.

'I'm sorry,' I said. 'That's not for me.'

'Mr Wormold?' one of the men asked.

'Yes,' I said.

'This is your television,' the man said. 'Look.' He had a paper in his hand with my name on it.

'OK,' I said. 'Come in.'

The men put the television in the living room and then left. It was a satellite television with television from all over the world.

I put the television on. There was American football on the television. I sat down in front of the television and watched the football.

There was a 'Ping!' from the computer. Chip was there. 'Come on, Frank,' she said. 'Let's do some more work.'

I wanted to watch more television, but Chip was right. I needed to work. I turned the television off and went back to the computer.

Chapter 5 *Help!*

At four o'clock I heard another noise at the door. Two men in white coats were there.

'Good afternoon, sir,' one of the men said. He gave me a piece of paper.

'Write your name here, please.'

I wrote my name.

'Thank you, sir,' the man said. 'Here are the keys.'

'Keys to what?' I asked.

'To your car, sir,' the man said. 'The car's outside.'

'Wow, a car!' I closed the door and ran to the window. I looked down. Outside the front door was a big new blue car. I went back to the computer and typed 'Help!'

Chip came on the screen. 'Can I help?' she asked.

'Yes,' I typed. 'Where did the television and car come from?'

'From me, but don't think about them now,' she said. 'Just write the book.'

'I want to see the car,' I typed.

'OK,' Chip said. 'But finish the book first.'

'No,' I said.

'Finish the book!' said Chip.

'No,' I shouted. 'I want to see the car.'

I put on a coat and went out into the lift. The lift doors closed. 'Sixth floor. Going down,' the lift said. 'How's the book going? Nearly finished?'

'Oh, be quiet!' I shouted.

When the lift stopped I ran out into the street.

I took out the keys and got into the car. I didn't drive anywhere. I just sat in the car. I turned the key and the car started. A voice said 'Hello. It is 18°C. The time is 4.15.' It was a talking car!

'Where do you want to go?' the car asked.

'I don't want to go anywhere,' I said.

'OK,' the car answered. The car could hear what I said! I turned the car off and got out. I went back to the lift and got in. 'Time to do some more writing,' the lift said.

'Yes, yes, OK.' I went into the flat. I sat down at the computer again and started to write. There was a 'Ping!' Chip came on the screen.

24

KING ALFRED'S COLLEGE
LIBRARY

'I did some work when you were out,' Chip said. 'I finished the book.'

'What!' I said to myself. Then I typed 'What?'

'I finished the book,' she said again. 'But I had to make some changes.'

'Changes?' I typed.

'Yes,' Chip said. 'I didn't like the name of the book. So I changed it.'

'You did what?' I typed.

'I changed the name of the book,' Chip said. 'Its new name is "Every Hour". Much nicer.'

'Why?' I typed. I was angry with Chip now. 'Any other changes?'

'Yes,' Chip said. 'The story is now about a young newspaper woman and the men she knows.'

'Oh no!' I typed. 'And the ending? How does the story finish?'

'It's very unhappy,' Chip said. 'All the men die.'

'That's terrible. No-one's going to like that ending,' I typed.

'Oh yes,' Chip said. 'Mel Parks likes it!'

'How do you know?' I typed.

'I e-mailed the book to Mel,' Chip said. 'He wants us to write another story now.'

'Us?' I typed.

'Yes,' Chip said. 'I like writing with you.'

Then I heard the telephone. It was Mel.

'Hi, Frank,' Mel said. 'Great story. I loved the ending. What's the next book called?'

'Next book?' I asked.

'Yeah,' Mel answered. 'I need another story by the weekend – about the same newspaper woman.'

'Mel,' I answered. 'I need time. I need to think. I write slowly. Writing isn't easy.'

'You've got Chip,' Mel said. 'And $200,000. How much do you want for the next book? Let's say half a million? OK?'

'OK, Mel,' I said and put the phone down.

I sat and looked at the screen for a long time. I was very unhappy now. I didn't want to write with a computer. A computer which changed everything I wrote. I liked writing by myself. I didn't want any more money – $200,000 was too much money anyway. And we now had a new car and a television. I didn't want to write for the movies any more.

I stood up. I knew what to do. I turned off the computer. Chip's face went from the screen. I left the room and went into the living room. I turned on the television. Chip's face was on the television screen.

'You can't turn me off like that,' Chip said. 'Now, about our next book. It's going to be about a writer. We're going to call it . . .'

'No,' I said and turned off the television.

I went back to the bedroom and picked up the computer. I had the computer in both hands and walked quickly out of the flat. I got into the lift.

'Sixth floor,' the lift said. 'Not going down. Put Chip back in the flat. Now!'

'No,' I shouted.

I ran out of the lift. Then I walked down the stairs to the street with the computer. I put the computer in the car and then I got in. I started the car.

26

'Hello,' the car said. 'It's 18°C. The time is 4.45. Where do you want to go?' the car asked.

'London Bridge,' I said.

'OK,' the car said. 'Take the A12.'

I drove quickly along the A12 to London Bridge. I stopped the car. Then I picked up the computer and tried to open the door, but I couldn't.

'Do not get out of the car,' the car said. 'The doors are closed. Put the computer down.'

I put the computer down. I sat and thought. Then I opened a window and threw the computer out. The computer fell into the water.

I started the car again.

'There,' I said. 'No computer now!'

'And no car,' said the car.

The car stopped. I tried and tried but I couldn't make it start. I got out and walked home. It was a long walk.

When I got home I walked up to the flat; I didn't want to use the lift. I was tired after the long walk. I sat down in the chair and went to sleep.

Chapter 6   *Teresa comes back*

'I'm here,' someone said. I opened my eyes. It was Teresa!

'Asleep!' Teresa said with a smile.

I looked at my watch. It said nine o'clock!

'What are you doing here?' I asked.

'I came back for my laptop computer,' Teresa answered. 'I need to have the laptop at work.'

'But that was yesterday!' I said.

'No,' Teresa answered. 'That was half an hour ago.'

'No, please listen,' I said. 'We're rich. I've got $200,000!'

Teresa looked at me. 'I don't know what you're talking about,' she said. 'I've got to go to work. I can't stay here listening to your stories.'

'But it's not a story,' I said. 'Please listen.'

Then I told Teresa about Mel Parks and MegaMonster Movies and about the computer, and the television and the car.

'Oh, yes,' she said. 'But where are the computer, and the television and the car?'

She was right. There was no computer or television in the living room.

'It was a dream,' Teresa said with a smile. 'Something you thought about when you were asleep.'

Teresa was right. There was no computer, no car, no MegaMonster, no Chip. Just a dream.

'But why?' I said. 'I don't usually dream about cars and computers and televisions.'

'I don't know,' said Teresa. 'But I don't have time to sit and talk about your dreams.' She was still angry with me.

'No, wait!' I said. 'I had the dream because you're not happy with me. Every morning you tell me to find another job so we can have a nice car and a better television. And I want you to be happy, so I dreamed we had all of those things.'

Teresa looked at me for a long time. Then she sat down next to me.

'Well, I think I understand now,' she said. 'A nice car and a new television are important. But you are much more important. And if you really want to be a writer then I am happy. I'm sorry.'

'Thank you,' I said. And we kissed. It was a long kiss. I was very happy. Teresa wasn't angry with me now.

'I must go to work,' said Teresa, 'but I just need to look at my e-mail to see if there are any messages.' Teresa turned on the laptop computer. The computer went 'ping'. There were no messages but I saw the word 'Help' on the screen.

'Look,' I said.

'What?' Teresa asked.

'"Help" on the screen,' I said.

'I don't see anything,' she said.

I closed my eyes. Then I heard a voice. A woman's voice. An American woman's voice.

'Help!' said the voice. 'Help!' I could hear water. It was Chip and she was in the water. 'Help!'

'I can't see anything,' Teresa said.

I opened my eyes. There was nothing on the screen.

'Did you hear anything?' I asked.

'No,' she said, 'it's all in your head.'

'Yes,' I said, 'it must be.'

'I've got an idea,' Teresa said. 'Why don't you write down the dream?'

'That's a good idea,' I said. 'Yes, it's a really good idea.'

'Now, I must go!' Teresa said again. She stood up and went to the door. This time she took the laptop computer. She looked beautiful. I knew she wasn't a dream.

'Thanks,' I said.

'Why?' asked Teresa.

'For the idea, for the help . . . for everything,' I said.

She smiled at me. Then she closed the door.

I got a notebook. Then I got my old pen and sat at the table. I wrote the first line of the story.

'I'm leaving now,' Teresa said . . .

KING ALFRED'S COLLEGE
LIBRARY